AF441984

My Greatest Joy

A Short Story Collection

Editor
SMITA VIVEK

Copyright © <2025> < Smita Vivek >

All Rights Reserved.

This book has been self-published with all reasonable efforts taken to make the material error-free by the editor. No part of this book shall be used, reproduced in any manner whatsoever without written permission from the editor, except in the case of brief quotations embodied in critical articles and reviews.

The authors of each story in this book are solely responsible and liable for their content including but not limited to the views, representations, descriptions, statements, information, opinions and references ["Content"]. The Content of this book shall not constitute or be construed or deemed to reflect the opinion or expression of the Publisher. The Publisher does not endorse or approve the Content of this book or guarantee the reliability, accuracy or completeness of the Content published herein and do not make any representations or warranties of any kind, express or implied, including but not limited to the implied warranties of merchantability, fitness for a particular purpose. The Publisher shall not be liable whatsoever for any errors, omissions, whether such errors or omissions result from negligence, accident, or any other cause or claims for loss or damages of any kind, including without limitation, indirect or consequential loss or damage arising out of use, inability to use, or about the reliability, accuracy or sufficiency of the information contained in this book.

Made with ❤ on the Notion Press Platform

www.notionpress.com

Contents

Preface

This anthology is dedicated to all those who have brought joy in our lives, or have helped us find joy within ourselves. This sense of utter satisfaction can come when we least expect it, or could be a result of a gruelling situation none of us would participate in voluntarily. But as life happens without our permission, it rewards us from time to time for reaching certain milestones in life.

All the stories I received through the Call for Submission, were beyond my expectation. Young minds and experienced, have given their unique understanding of what joy means to them. These stories depict that joy can

CONTENTS

come from various places, in various forms. Coincidently all of them revolve around women. These narratives touch upon various aspects of being a woman— love, anger, dejection, growth, joy, etc.

Many a times, joy comes as a validation and sometimes just a reminder of what life is supposed to be like. Reminding us the importance of just living in the present. Reflecting on how our present is a result of whatever happened in the past or our past actions. Instead of regretting, we get to look at our lives collectively to find meaning.

-   Dr. Smita Vivek
    Editor

Acknowledgments

I would like to thank my family for their support and for believing in me. A special thanks to my daughter, who is the force that pushes me to work harder each day.

I would like to extend my gratitude to all the contributors who trusted me with their stories and worked hard on making the improvements suggested during the process.

Finally, I would like to thank you for choosing to spend your time reading these stories. Hope you are inspired enough to contribute in my upcoming collection.

Smita Vivek

One

Echoes of Solitude: Embracing the Silence

About The Author

Ms. Swetha Dhantal is a dedicated emotional freedom life coach based in Austin, Texas, specializing in Neuro-Linguistic Programming (NLP). With a background in neuro-cognitive and counselling psychology, Swetha passionately guides individuals through their journey to emotional freedom and personal growth. She is the founder of The Conversation Nook, a coaching practice focused on helping clients navigate life transitions, manage emotional triggers, and achieve a deeper sense of self-awareness and resilience.

Swetha's approach is rooted in her commitment to empowering others to master their emotional experiences and embrace their authentic selves. She combines her professional expertise with her personal experiences as a mother and her love for science fiction to bring a unique perspective to her work. An advocate for lifelong learning and self-improvement, Swetha is dedicated to making a meaningful impact through her coaching, workshops, and speaking engagements. When she's not working, she enjoys reading self-help books and exploring new ideas to enrich her practice and life.

CONTENTS

"Echoes of Solitude: Embracing the Silence"

- Swetha Dhantal

March 21st, 2016. A crisp Monday morning in Delaware, USA. The sun was just beginning to peek through the blinds, casting long shadows across the bare walls of our small apartment. I was at the stove, scrambling eggs, the sizzle, and pop of the pan blending with the low hum of the radio. My husband, fresh out of the shower, was in the next room gathering his essentials—a brown leather briefcase, a neatly folded blazer, a pair of polished shoes that clicked against the hardwood floor. The air was filled with the scent of coffee and the unspoken promise of a new beginning.

We sat down for breakfast, a simple meal of toast, eggs, and tea. There wasn't much conversation; we were both lost in our thoughts.

"I can't believe it's only been four days," he said, breaking the silence. "Feels like we've been here forever."

I looked up, trying to muster a smile. "It does feel like a lot has happened already."

He nodded, pouring himself a cup of coffee. "I know it's a lot to take in. Are you doing okay?"

I hesitated, then nodded. "Yeah, just a little overwhelmed. It's a big change, you know?"

He reached across the table, squeezing my hand gently. "You'll get used to it. We've got this."

After breakfast, he stood up, grabbed his bag, and walked toward the door. He turned back for a moment, gave me a quick smile, and then kissed me on the cheek. "See you tonight," he said, his voice filled with the comfort of familiarity.

I smiled back, but inside, my heart was racing. "See you tonight."

As the door clicked shut, I was left standing in the middle of the room, surrounded by silence. The silence was new, unfamiliar. It was as if the apartment, in all its emptiness, was holding its breath, waiting for something to happen. This was my first week in the USA, and the adventure I had dreamed of was just beginning. I had only been here four days, and already, everything was falling into place—or so I thought.

***

Let me take you back for a moment, to where it all began.

I was born in Mumbai, a city that never sleeps, a city where life is a constant buzz of activity, where every corner tells a story. My world was a whirlwind of colour, sound, and movement—a cacophony of voices, opinions, and laughter that I thrived in. I grew up in a joint family, surrounded by uncles, aunts, cousins, and grandparents. There was always someone to talk to, always something happening. Our home was a vibrant tapestry of traditions, festivals, and celebrations, where the lines between individual and collective were blurred, where life was lived in the company of others.

From an early age, I learned to navigate this sea of personalities and emotions. I was the girl who could strike up a conversation with anyone, who could make friends in an instant, who thrived in the chaos of social interaction. I was an extrovert to my core—a social butterfly who was comfortable in any setting, who found joy in the energy and presence of others. I loved the noise, the chatter, the opinions, and the endless conversations that filled every moment of my life.

School, too, was a social affair. I was sent to boarding school at the age of 11, and for the next decade, I lived in close quarters with dozens of other girls. We shared everything—our rooms, our meals, our dreams, our fears. The dormitories were always alive with whispers, giggles, and the occasional outburst of teenage drama. I was never alone, not even for a moment. And I loved it. I thrived in that environment, where there was always someone to talk to, always something happening.

After school, I went on to college and then to graduate school, all the while surrounded by people, by friends who became family, by professors who became mentors. I moved from one bustling city to another, from one lively campus to the next. My life was a series of shared experiences, of collective moments that were loud, vibrant, and full of life. This was all I knew, and I embraced it with open arms.

And then, in 2016, I got married and moved to the USA. It was a dream come true. The prospect of a new life in a new country filled me with excitement and anticipation. I imagined myself building a career, making new friends, and embracing the adventure of married life. I was so prepared for it all—working hard, earning money, managing a home, building a family. I knew it wouldn't be easy, but I was ready. I had seen my parents juggle work and family with grace, and I was confident I could do the same. I was an extrovert, talkative, loud, opinionated—a woman who was comfortable in her skin, ready to take on the world.

***

But that morning, as I stood in the middle of our apartment, the silence began to creep in. My husband had left for work, and I realized that I had the entire day to myself. There was nothing on my schedule, nothing demanding my attention. I wasn't yet allowed to work, as my work permit visa was still being processed. So, I did what I thought I should—I cleaned the apartment, made the bed, tidied up the kitchen, and folded the laundry. But it didn't take long; after all, there wasn't much in the apartment. A couch, a small kitchen, a mattress— barely enough to fill the space.

I walked from room to room, checking off tasks in my mind, but the sense of accomplishment I was used to didn't come. Instead, I felt an unfamiliar weight settle in the pit of my stomach. I glanced at the clock. It was only 11 AM. Something felt off. The hands of the clock seemed to move slower than usual, as if time itself had decided to stretch out, to make the minutes feel like hours. I checked my phone, the microwave, even my wristwatch. Time was moving, but it felt like it was standing still. The apartment began to feel vast and empty, the walls closing in on me.

I tried to distract myself. I turned on the TV, but the noise felt intrusive, grating against the silence that had settled in the room. I turned it off. I picked up a book, but the words blurred on the page, my mind too restless to focus. I put the book down. I played some music, but even that felt wrong—too loud, too forced, too much. I turned it off.

I walked to the window and looked outside. The world was moving, people were going about their day, cars were driving by, birds were chirping, the sun was shining. But inside, it was just me. Just me and the silence.

And then, out of nowhere, I heard it—the rhythmic ticking of the clock on the wall. It was a sound I had never noticed before, a sound that had always been drowned out by the noise of life. But now, that was all I could hear. Tick. Tock. Tick. Tock. The sound echoed in the empty room, a constant reminder of the passage of time, of the minutes slipping by, of the hours stretching out before me.

I felt a wave of panic rise in my chest. I grabbed the edge of the futon, trying to steady myself. *"What is happening?"* I whispered to the empty room. The apartment, which started off as a place of comfort, now felt like a cage, a prison of my own making. The walls seemed to close in, the silence pressing down on me, suffocating me. I realized, in that moment, that I was truly and utterly alone.

I had never felt this kind of loneliness before. It wasn't just the absence of people; it was the absence of everything I had ever known. The absence of noise, of conversation, of the comforting hum of life. I was alone with my thoughts, with no distractions, no voices to guide me, to tell me what to do or how to feel. It was just me, and the ticking of the clock.

I sat down on the futon, my mind racing. I tried to fight it, to push the loneliness away, but it clung to me, wrapping itself around me like a heavy blanket. I felt tears welling up in my eyes, but I didn't let them fall. I didn't want to admit it, didn't want to acknowledge that this was how I felt. I was supposed to be strong, supposed to be excited about this new life. But all I felt was empty, lost in a sea of silence.

I don't know how long I sat there, staring at the clock, watching the minutes tick. But in that silence, something began to shift. I started to notice things I had never noticed before—the sound of my own breath, the rhythm of my heartbeat, the way the light filtered through the curtains, casting soft shadows on the floor. I began to feel the weight of my own presence, the reality of being alone with myself.

And then, in the midst of that silence, a thought came to me—a thought that had been buried deep beneath the noise of my life— "What if this wasn't something to be feared?" I mused aloud. "What if this silence, this solitude, was a gift?"

In that moment, I realized something profound. *Solitude wasn't just the absence of others—it was the presence of myself.* It was a space where I could truly be me, without the distractions, without the noise, without the opinions of others. It was a chance to reconnect with who I was, to rediscover myself in a way I had never done before.

And so, I decided to embrace it. I decided to use this time to explore the person I had become, to understand what I wanted from this new chapter of my life. I started to create a plan, to set goals for myself, to think about what I wanted to achieve. I began to write, to journal, to express my thoughts and feelings on paper. I reached out to friends and family back home, finding comfort in their voices, their words, their support.

As the days went by, I started to find my rhythm. I discovered the joys of cooking, of exploring new recipes and flavours. I found solace in long walks through the neighbourhood, in the quiet moments of reflection that came with each step. I started to build a routine, a structure for my days that helped me feel grounded and purposeful.

And slowly, the loneliness began to fade. It was replaced by a sense of peace, of contentment. I realized that being alone didn't mean being isolated—it meant being free. Free to explore, to grow, to discover who I was and what I wanted from life. It was a journey, a process of self-discovery that would continue to unfold with each passing day.

Looking back, I see now that this was a turning point in my life. It was a moment when I began to understand the true meaning of emotional freedom. It wasn't about being constantly surrounded by others, or about being busy and active all the time. It was about finding peace within myself, about being comfortable in my own skin, about embracing the silence and solitude as opportunities for growth and self-discovery.

Today, I am still an extrovert, still talkative, still opinionated. But I am also someone who values solitude, who finds strength and clarity in those quiet moments of self-reflection. I have learned that true emotional freedom comes from within, from the ability to be at peace with myself, to find joy and contentment in my own company.

And so, the story that began with the discomfort of silence ends with the embrace of solitude. The fear of being alone has transformed into the joy of self-discovery, the anxiety of loneliness into the peace of emotional freedom. It's a journey I never expected to take, but one that has led me to a deeper understanding of myself, and a more authentic way of living.

Two

Echoes of Laughter

About The Author

Ms. Sindhu Prasanthi Dasu is a storyteller who finds joy in exploring the complexities of human emotions and relationships. Her experiences living in various parts of the world have broadened her understanding of diverse cultures and perspectives, infusing her stories with a blend of traditional and modern themes. She loves crafting narratives that offer a fresh and authentic voice. When she isn't writing, she enjoys immersing herself in books, discovering new places, and spending quality time with her family.

Echoes of Laughter

- Sindhu Prasanthi Dasu

The familiar tune of *Amma donga ninnu chudakunte naku benga*, a song by Palagummi Viswanatham that translates to "My mischievous one, I feel restless when I can't see you," floated softly through the house, a poignant reminder of what was missing. I paused outside my mother's door, the song echoing her feelings of longing. It had been weeks since my sister and her family left, and the house still felt unnervingly quiet.

Pushing open the door, I found Amma seated by the window, clutching a blanket that once belonged to her granddaughter. "*Amma donga ninnu chudakunte naku benga,*" she sang softly, her voice trembling. Her eyes, filled with unshed tears, looked out into the distance, as if willing them to return.

"Amma," I said gently, taking a seat beside her. "I miss them too."

The house had been vibrant just a short while ago. It all began on a morning filled with the scent of incense and the soothing sounds of the Sri Venkateswara Suprabhatam. I had woken up in a panic, realizing we needed to get to the airport soon. My mother, already serene and prepared, reassured me with a calm smile, "Relax. Everything will be fine. This is a special day."

Indeed, it was special. My sister was visiting for the first time since her marriage and the birth of her child. Mom had been unable to travel for the delivery, and now, after months of anticipation, she was finally meeting her grandchild.

We decorated the house with balloons and colorful banners, a nameplate ready to welcome them.

At the airport, the moment Mom held the baby, tears welled in her eyes. "You're even more beautiful than I imagined," she whispered. The baby's innocent smile seemed to bridge the gap of months apart, forging an immediate and deep bond.

The days that followed were filled with joy. Every giggle and coo were a treasure for Mom. "This little one brings so much light into my life," she often said. Traditional rituals, like the tonsure and ear-piercing ceremonies, were organized with great care. For Mom, these were not just customs but symbols of love and new beginnings.

One afternoon, while sitting with the baby, Mom confided, "I've always loved children, but this one is different. All the love I've ever felt seems wrapped up in this tiny bundle of joy."

But as always, time moved forward, and the inevitable goodbye approached. The day of departure came, and the baby's smile, though warm, was tinged with sadness. We waved until the car was out of sight, and upon returning home, the quiet felt heavy and hollow. The absence of the baby's laughter left a void that was impossible to fill.

Mom tried to maintain a brave front, but I often found her retreating to her room, closing the door softly behind her. I discovered her tears during these moments of solitude, and one evening, I heard her humming the song that captured her heartache: "I feel restless when I can't see you."

"We knew they had to go," she said to me later, her voice breaking. "But I miss that little bundle of joy more than I imagined."

I hugged her tightly. "We'll see them again soon. Until then, we'll hold on to these precious memories."

We found comfort in replaying those cherished moments. The house, though quiet, was alive with the anticipation of their return. Mom's greatest joy—her grandchild—would eventually return, filling the home with laughter once more.

In the quiet moments, Mom often reflected, "No matter where life takes us, the joy of holding that little one and seeing her smile is something I'll carry with me always. She's not just my granddaughter, she's my greatest joy, my little piece of heaven on earth."

And so, we wait, hearts full of love and a home ready to be filled with laughter again, knowing that the greatest joy will return, bringing warmth and happiness only a grandchild can provide.

Three

Our Fond Fairy

About The Author

Mr. Janardhan Amballa has about 54 years of Managerial experience in Banking and Finance and 30 years of experience with Literature. He worked with various banks like the Union Bank Of India, Bombay Mercantile Co-op. Bank Ltd., Pressman Corporate Group, Cosmos Co-op. Bank Ltd. and Dewan Housing Finance Corporation Ltd. For the last Seventeen years, he is working as a freelance financial consultant. He has published 19 books of fiction, essays and poetry in Telugu, English, Hindi, Marathi, and Odia. He is also a translator working with languages such as English, Telugu, Marathi, Hindi and Gujarati. He is attached to many Social, Cultural and Literary organisations in Mumbai and Telangana.

Our Fond Fairy

- Janardhan Amballa

It was the annual day celebrations of a Foreign Bank with Indian Operations. The A.C. hall in Mumbai, with more than 2000 persons capacity was full, with Bank's staff and their family members. We were there, as parents of our youngest daughter, who worked for the said Bank.

The gathering had people from different parts of India. This celebration gained importance since the C.E.O. of Asia Operations, who is stationed at Singapore was delivering a keynote address on the expansion plans of the Bank, in the Asia Region. He would also declare "Best Employee" of the year.

The Bank had also organised some cultural events, so their employees could engage with talents other than their banking skills. Some sang, while some others danced. Some cut jokes and some recited "Shero Shayrees" in Hindi. Our daughter Aparna (Appoo) played Krishna in the "all ladies ballet of Radha Krishna Leela."

This was followed by the Anchor announcing names of the five nominations for "Best Employee" of the year ended 31st December of the previous year. She then requested the CEO to announce the winner.

The CEO asked the audience to guess the winner. Many people shouted some names. After a little hype and creating suspense, he announced "*Best Employee of the year is ...*" and he paused for effect. The curiosity of the audience knew no bounds. They, including me and my wife put our fingers crossed and waited for the big announcement.

Finally, the CEO announced *"Aparna Anumalla."* We just couldn't believe our ears. It was our "Appoo" our own daughter, *Our Fond Fairy*, who was bestowed with such a prestigious honour. The CEO in his keynote address, outlined the progress of Asia Region and congratulated the staff for their contribution towards progress of the Bank Operations. He also spelt out development plans for the ensuing years. While dwelling on the same, he made special mention of Ms Aparna Anumalla (Our Appoo) and how her out-of-the-box thinking led to the progress of the Bank. Instead of waiting for the High Networth individuals to come to the Bank, Aparna, with the help of her contacts, went to their office with prior appointment and made them shift their Banking Operations to this Bank. She also made presentations in the Local Chamber of Commerce and explained USP of our Bank, which brought sizable business to the Bank. Not only did she do her job efficiently without watching the clock, but she also enhanced the Bank's reputation by designing and participating in the Corporate Social Responsibility (CSR) programmes undertaken by the Bank.

He wished her best for her future career and announced a promotion as well. He said so many good things about our daughter. My happiness was such that everything he said slowly faded into the background and all my focus was on my child who was receiving such great words. I was just so proud of our Fond Fairy.

After receiving her award, our daughter addressed the gathering. This time, I heard each and every word she said,

"I thank the management for the confidence bestowed upon me and assure that I will continue to work for the overall development of the Bank, with new vigour and enthusiasm. Though this honour is bestowed upon me, it is due to the efforts of all our team members, that we could perform so well. I dedicate this award to my parents who have made me what I am today. It is because of the values they inculcated in me that I could work with such devotion and dedication. They are here and I see them gleaming. If I may add here, I have a few suggestions for increasing the Bank's share of business in the Asian Region. I will be writing about them to the Management. Thank you again for this honour. It means a lot."

As soon as our daughter finished her speech,

As we were returning with the Award, from the dais, many people thronged us to congratulate and offer best wishes. It took almost twenty minutes for us to come to our seats. Our Appoo fell at our feet and sought our blessings. Our eyes were full with tears of Joy.

During the lunch, we met the CEO personally. We had a cordial interaction. But he said something during that meeting. He said, "thank you for bringing such a wonderful person into the worlds." I simply smiled and the night went on.

In Telugu, there is a poem in Sumati Shatakam, written by Baddena Kavi:

పుత్రోత్సాహము తండ్రికి పుత్రుడు జన్మించినపుడు పుట్టదు, జనులా పుత్రుని కనుగొని పొగడగ పుత్రోత్సాహంబు నాడు పొందుర సుమతీ...!

Meaning, it is common for a father to be happy at the birth of a son, but he will be truly and extremely happy when his son is praised by people for his accomplishments.

Though the above poem refers to birth of a son, and happiness of a father, it is equally applicable to birth of a daughter and happiness of a mother. In these days, women are competing with men in all fields, there is no much distinction between sons and daughters. Further, mothers have equal responsibility in the upbringing of children. In fact, they play a major role in carving better personalities out of their progeny. In the times of Baddena Kavi, women were not as vibrant as today, but were confined to the four walls of the house. Hence, the reference in the above poem is to son and father only. It is but natural for us to be elated at the achievement of our Fond Fairy.

That night was over, but the CEO's words stayed with me. It coxed me to reflect on our lives since Appoo entered our lives. Before Appoo, we already had a daughter and a son then. Those were the days of "*Hum do, hamare do*" meaning "We two, ours Two," as spelt out by the then Government. So, we were confused about a third issue. After we realised my wife was pregnant again, we discussed at length on whether to keep the third one or to abort it. After deliberations for about a month, we decided to throw the ball into the court of my Parents and my in-Laws. Since we thought it was not advisable to seek their opinion on phone, we decided to go personally to our native State where they lived. But as the distance between their houses in our Native State was about five hundred kms, we needed a minimum of one week's leave. Getting the leave itself for both of us was a different problem. By the time we went to our native place, my wife was already in the fifth month of pregnancy, which meant abortion at this stage would be risky for her life as well.

Nevertheless, we went to my parents and sought their advice on the matter. On hearing our query, they literally pounced upon us. It was natural for them since they reared seven children, despite limited means and my father being the only earning member for the family.

"Don't you see how we brought you and six of your brethren up?" My father thundered at me. "You people, for the sake of mortal comforts, both work and don't want to beget more children. Even the limited children you give birth to, you leave them at the mercy of Ayahs or baby care centres. We didn't resort to such things, but personally brought you all up with the best traditions of our culture and heritage.

"But you want to enjoy your family life, which led to conceiving and now you don't want to keep it as it will result in additional responsibilities of its upbringing." My mother quipped.

We had no answers for them. Undeterred, we went to our in-law's place. On hearing our dilemma, they too voiced the same opinion as my parents. They had eight children! So, it was natural for them to give such advice.

We were doubly sure that we should keep the third child, irrespective of the fact that it would be a boy or a girl. Now it is illegal, but in our times, we could get a Sonography to know the gender of the baby. Not that we went for it, we just wanted a healthy baby. That is how Appoo came into this world.

We named her Aparna, another name of Goddess Parvathi. It means the one who is strong-willed and can endure great challenges to achieve what her heart desires. What an apt name for the woman she turned out to be. We looked after her very well, just like our elder two children. We sent her to the best school in the vicinity, and encouraged her to participate in extracurricular activities. We gave her the freedom to choose her vocation and she excelled in Electronics and Telecommunications Engineering. It was no surprise that, she got a good pay package in the present Foreign Bank, in their Campus recruitment. And now she made us proud by her dedication to her assignments and being adjudged as Best Employee.

She actively participated in welfare schemes undertaken by the Bank, under Corporate Social Responsibility (CSR), stipulated by the Government. Probably that must have been a major factor for choosing her as the "Best Employee." Going out of her way and making the choices she made with regards to her work and CSR needs confidence; and more than that intensions.

As they say, daughters are more attached to fathers and sons are more attached to mothers. It is true in my case too. My Appoo confides more in me than her mother. My wife, who is more demanding, tries to control our children, lest they fall prey to bad company and habits. On the other hand, I am more liberal and easily accede to the demands of our children. My wife doesn't like it. But our children and I don't care. We feel that she is addicted to old tradition of burqua and pardah.

After her intermediate exams, my daughter said, "Amma! Let's go to our native place for change of climate and surroundings. I want to refresh myself after all the stress I underwent for my exams. I also want to spend some time with my grandparents, want to breathe fresh air of the countryside and have insights into village life."

My wife consulted me and told me that she would not get leave from office. Same thing was true in my case. So, we decided to explain our predicament to Appoo.

"Beta! It is very difficult for the both of us to get leave. Even your elder brother and sister cannot accompany you since they are having their final exams. Let's us go to our native place some other time."

"Papa! It's okay, I can go alone. Once my results are out, I will be busy trying for admissions in a good professional course and then with my studies for the same. I want to rejuvenate myself before being busy in my higher studies."

"How can we send a grown-up girl alone? These days many untoward incidents are taking place, especially with young girls," my wife put her foot down.

My daughter looked at me for help. I could understand her position. As usual I supported our Appoo. With great persuasion, my wife agreed to send our daughter alone to our Parents and in-Laws. However, she used to phone Appoo every day and ask about her wellbeing.

During her engineering course, my daughter wanted to go on a study-tour planned by her college authorities. Again, my wife refused to give her permission. She said to me "How can we allow a grown-up girl to be away for so long, with boy students who were also participants of the tour, that too for a full week? Let her learn whatever they are supposed to learn, from the available books. God knows what will happen tomorrow."

As it was a co-education college, my wife's apprehensions were understandable. My daughter again sought my indulgence.

She said, "Papa! Our senior Lecturers and Professors would be there to ensure discipline amongst us and will ensure that nothing goes wrong. Such study-tours are common in colleges and in the history of our college nothing, objectionable happened in the past."

I intervened again and tried to convince my wife that these days children have to mingle with the other gender for education and work. At the same time, they know how to protect themselves from untoward incidents. Further, there are teachers to control the students. After great persuasion, my wife ceded. That incident brought my Appoo closer to me. There were more such incidents.

Once my daughter wanted us to buy jeans and tee-shirts as was the fashion amongst her friends at college. My wife got furious at the thought. "How can girls dress like boys leaving chest open?" They should either wear sarees or choodidars, with palloos.

Again, I intervened and convinced my wife that our daughter should be allowed to have her say, since I have full confidence in her that she will not go awry.

As final exams were coming closer, during the preparatory holidays, our daughter said,

"Papa! I want to go to my friend's place for combined studies, as it would be easier to clear each other's doubts. They stay across the street and there is nobody to disturb us. I will return by six p.m."

My wife who was standing beside me intervened "Nothing doing. Even in our house nobody would disturb you, so why do you want to go elsewhere?" My daughter helplessly looked at me. I told her to be calm and that I will talk to her mother later.

In the night my wife confided with me in private, "Dear! Please understand why I am against Appoo going out in the name of combined studies. Have you not heard of girls going out on such pretext and going elsewhere with their boyfriends? Many times, it so happens that girls fall in love with the brother of their friends and go out of control. In these days of many such atrocities being committed by teenage girls, we should take extra care in protecting our daughter."

I explained "Dear! such incidents are rare and our daughter, with Black belt under her belt, is capable of handling any such eventualities. Such incidents will not happen to our daughter as she is capable of setting her priorities. Moreover, the classmate to whose house she wants to go for combined studies has no brother, and she is right across the street and not too far. She is dedicated to her studies and I am sure that she will not dither from her goal. Even the police force has constituted "SHE TEAMS" to protect women against such incidents." It was only after such detailed assurance that my wife relented and allowed our daughter to go out for combined studies.

Just like me, our Appoo is a multi-tasker. She engages herself in social work, during her holidays. Once she led her team to a Municipal girls School to teach the students there about Good Touch and Bad Touch. She focused on Ninth and Tenth class girl, as she felt they are most vulnerable due to their age. These are the girls who will soon be going to college or out in the world for jobs. While counselling them on the subject, she explained how the girls should deal with Bad Touch. She spread awareness about all the authorities whom the girls could contact in case of emergency or reporting someone. She also advised them to learn Karate and Kung fu, which will help them in self-defence. All the girls profusely thanked my daughter for enlightening them on the subject. Even the teachers showed their gratitude as some of them wanted to discuss these topics, but were uncomfortable due to their circumstances.

She is a District President of Toast Masters club, which is engaged in organising various lectures and public speaking sessions. In short, with her leadership qualities, she made her mark in various social work activities. When Appoo went to a Government Nursery school and engaged the children with various Games. The children flocked to her and insisted her to come daily and play with them. She even prefers celebrating her birthdays at Anathashrams (orphanage) and Vruddhashrams (homes for the aged). Her logic is, she gets to spend each day with people who love her and whom she loves. But there are so many who crave love, and if she can share a bit of love with them on her birthday, it makes her feel fulfilled.

She has grown up to be an independent woman, in its truest sense. She holds a senior position at a Multinational Bank; and though junior-most, she acts like our mother at home. She does her share of the household chores, ensures that I have taken my medicines on time, and even scolds us if we miss our daily walk or indulge in eating anything unhealthy.

The CEO thanked us for bringing her into the world, but we thank the universe for gifting us this precious bundle of joy. We would have really missed her had we gone for nipping her in the bud.

Four

Quintessentially Divine

About The Author

Ms. Jessica Louis is a Research Scholar and an Assistant Professor in the Department of English in a private college at Trichy, Tamil Nadu. Her areas of Interest lie in Nature, Love, Divinity and Literature. Currently she is pursuing her Research on Cross Cultural Feminism in Nigerian and Indian American Writers. She has written few Confessional and Devotional poems and has published a short story titled *One Day my Dream Would Come True* in an E- Anthology. She loves to explore the world and associate with novel experiences and people. Her passion is to teach varied students and inculcate ethical values and shape them into better human beings.

Quintessentially Divine

- **Jessica Louis**

We rushed to the hospital. His pupils dilated, saliva drooling, feet turned blue. He was motionless in my arms. We rushed to the children's ward. The doctors fixed the saline and oxygen mask. The nurses were doing their best to revive him. But finally, we were asked to take him to a bigger hospital which had better equipment and worked with such advanced cases. The greatest joy of my life was just another case which they could not handle.

When he hired my womb, I never thought that he would become my lot. Everything that belonged to him was a part of me. The fragrance of his skin, the beating of his heart, the whispers of his breath, everything created a divine connection between us. He was my eldest son. He was my companion in ebb and flow of life. His presence was enough to make my life better, no matter how horrible the situation.

Have you heard the saying, "a woman's life is full of paradoxes?" My life was not far away from that quote. I had gone to the doctor because of a prolonged illness. I had fever, body ache and nausea. But as it turned out, I was actually pregnant. I will never forget that moment though. As I looked at the pregnancy test, my eyes flooded, and my words drowned. I started praying more intensely. And one morning, as I prayed, I heard a voice from the depth of my heart, "giftson." After that day, I heard this word frequently during various prayer sessions, I believed that God is about to gift me a baby boy. And I knew this child was gifted to me for a special reason.

April 9th, 2016- God, what a day that was! The doctors said I had completed my term and we had to induce false labour to avoid any risks. In that situation, all you want to do is deliver a healthy baby, so you listen to the doctors, don't you? They injected me at 11:30 am, and I was monitored closely since. After almost eleven hours of nothing but pain and bleeding, the doctors realised that the baby is stuck. The umbilical cord held the baby by the throat. Can you imagine what it feels to receive such a terrible news! The connection between the baby and me, the one link that has been providing the nourishment to my child, is now entangled around its neck, putting my baby in danger. I could take a sigh of relief only after they finally delivered my baby at 11:25 pm.

I, myself, was admitted in the ICU due to the complications. But all the pain and discomfort subsided when my mother gave my baby boy in my hands. It was such a priceless moment, meeting this tiny man who has been growing inside of me for the past few months. His cute little arms and legs and lips and nose and ears. What a blessing!

We named him Jeshurun Yanis (Jeshurun meaning Upright and Yanis meaning God is Gracious). He was after all a gift of God. But soon I understood why this blessing felt more like a calling. Every mother loves their child, but being there for a special child needs a lot more than love. My boy was a light skinned bubbly boy with pink lips, but he could barely see, hear, feel, or taste. His joints were not steady even after months, and he had a squint. His motor skills development was delayed and his psychomotor skills were deteriorating. This child, who was still the best part of me, was diagnosed to have Cerebral Palsy.

He was spotted with one disorder, but I read about everything I needed to know about Cerebral Palsy, Autism, Spasticity and Down Syndrome. I just wanted to be informed in every way possible so that I can make my child's life comfortable. For many in the world, such special children are just disfigured bodies, or a curse because of their mother's sin, and what not. But for mothers like me, such children are a divine responsibility. He could have been anybody's child, but God chose me for the responsibility. And Yanis was never just a responsibility, he was my greatest joy.

There is no permanent cure or solution for his problems. There is no medicine that could ease his pain, or strengthen his joints, or make him see clearly. And as a caregiver, mothers like me usually don't have emotional support, or any kind words or even a shoulder to cry on. It is mostly rude comments and not-so-helpful advice coming our way. So, I had to make myself strong for the both of us. I took him to a special school every day. Thankfully the teachers and the physical therapist were good and kind.

Yanis liked the school, I could tell. He was mostly bound to the bed, so he could not participate like the other children. He could not sit, stand, dance, sing or even make eye contact. But he was happy there. Because he felt loved and valued. What made me strong, also broke me each day. But seeing him happy, was great encouragement. Like I said earlier, a woman's life is full of paradoxes.

But all places were not like his school. He faced hostility quite often. He was called many names and was treated like a curse. When he was six months old, and still appeared to be cute, people welcomed his presence. But as he turned one and then two and then three, people did not want a child that age to cling onto his mother like his life depended on it. But what they failed to see is that, his life did depend on others especially the mother. He could not eat like other children of his age, or explore the world with curiosity. Yanis needed me around to survive each day. And no one could convince me to do anything other than being there for my child.

I was bombarded with questions like, "why is he always in bed?" "Why can't he be like other kids?" "Eat fast. I can't hold him any longer, my hands are hurting." "Why is he so dumb?" All these comments hit my heart hard, but what hurt me most was that one Christmas evening, I was strictly asked to leave him alone in his bedroom while there was a Christmas gathering with celebrations and carols in the living room. I caved that night, under the pressure from my family members "what will people think about us?" He was all alone, locked in his room, and I was there with others as they celebrated.

I did not leave my child like that ever again. The next Christmas, I convinced them to let him be a spectator.

Just being in the room made him happy. Such was my boy. Happy with whatever came his way.

When covid hit, he could not attend school or go for physical therapy. So, I had to be more than his mother. It is said that a mother is the best therapist, a mother's touch and voice has healing powers for the child. I learnt whatever was needed from his teacher and therapist. I know I was only half as good as them at the job, but I did my best. Being confined to home, meant the intensity of comments that came my way grew stronger. But he was there for me, my greatest gift, my greatest joy. And with time, our connection grew stronger.

When Yanis turned four, I decided to prepare a birthday cake. I knew he could not blow the candles, use a knife to cut the cake, or even eat it. But I wanted my special boy to experience a special birthday. I went all in, made a bourbon cake, arranged candles, decorated the room and we had a blast. I am happy I did that.

Because soon we had to rush to the hospital. The doctors were busy handling covid patients. My child did not have covid and being a special child, he needed special attention, which they could not provide. The doctors asked us to take him to a better hospital, with doctors who knew how to handle his case. But it was too late. By the time I reached his bed side, the nurse told us he is *no more*.

I knew my son would not live a full life. But 4 and quarter years felt too less. Maybe a better hospital or better staff could have handled my pregnancy and delivery better. Maybe then Yanis could have lived a different life. Maybe taking him to a better hospital when he first became serious would have saved him or maybe he would have lived a little longer. There are many such doubts and questions that haunt me even today. But an inner voice reminds me about how this was destiny. He was and will also be my *Giftson*, My Greatest Joy in life.

Five

My Dear Father

About The Author

Ms. Anushka Pandit is a literature enthusiast with a love for storytelling and arts. Wondering how a BTech in Computer Science and Engineering from VIT-AP University relates to writing? Well, she is probably a writer, secretly! "My Dear Father" is their first published story as an author, which is a very big step in their literary life. Outside the realm of code and coursework, Anushka's love for reading across genres draws inspiration found within the pages of countless books. This story takes their journey a step forward and reflects their quest to balance the tangible and the abstract, offering readers a glimpse into their evolving perspective as they navigate life and literature.

My Dear Father

- Anushka Pandit

"The greatest joy of my life" - When I ponder upon this, it becomes an interesting question. Juggling through the calm and chaos of life, the definition of joy has become a little blurred when thought of explicitly and to mention the greatest joy is more of a challenge than the recollection of an intriguing story. Yet, I believe I know a path to discover it – A path that we all have traversed at least once in our lives, called Love.

Consider the road not taken or the one avoided out of fear of the unknown. Did we choose correctly when we took the path of reason? Or was it fear that guided us?

Reflecting on love, I see how it has shaped my journey towards finding joy. Love, in its many forms, has taken me on a tumultuous adventure. So, sit back, cue in some soft piano tunes, let the light drizzle of rainfall on our faces and serenity fill the environment as we get transferred to a decade and a half back because the transmission is the only time we'll have peace. The road we took is a rocky one, my friend. It's filled with unexpected turns and challenges.

***

It was quite dark outside when she looked out of the window, the dark, roaring clouds had rained and left the sky clear. She peeked outside the window to see the main road, the only one in her small town but saw no signs of her husband. She had prepared the dinner a while back and now sat awaiting her husband holding her toddler close to her heart. Her child was scared of the dark and she had nothing to offer but a dim lit candle. She rocked him to sleep, telling him stories of a little prince and counted stars for him. He, with his shiny two teeth, couldn't even count till two yet. She had just put her baby on the bed when she heard the horn blare.

She rushed to open the door and there he was. He reeked of alcohol. She lowered her eyes and said, "I was just waiting for you, how…" Her sentence was cut short by a slap that almost blacked her out for a minute.

"You dare ask me about my whereabouts, you lowly bitch!" Another slap followed but she had become numb by now. He caught hold of her hand and before she could register, she was being dragged inside. "You need to be taught a lesson, had your beggar father..." *No, my father is not a beggar!!!* she wanted to shout, *you took lakhs in dowry, you are the beggar!! He isn't!!* Her mind was a whirlwind of fear and helplessness. Every sense was heightened, every hurled abuse at her amplified and ran through her backbone. Every bruise on her body as she was being dragged was a searing reminder of the absolute torture her life was. She could only sob.

He threw her on the bed and her dignity was shredded with every piece of clothing he tore off her body, and every cuss he uttered as he did that. She kept quiet as tears fell from her eyes. She couldn't cry out loud; her baby was sleeping next to them. What if he woke up?

The monster pushed away from her and kicked her down the bed, "go bring me food, you cunt... You belong to the roads!" he said while dressing up. She swallowed her pain as she limped back to the kitchen, the food sat cold, like she was. She reheated and served him dinner. After all, it wasn't the first time this happened, it wouldn't be the last.

A few months later, she realised she was expecting again. She felt a knot tighten inside her gut little by little as the fact dawned upon her, the knot tightened till she couldn't breathe, not just by the anticipation of a life growing inside her but from the uncertainty that now clouded her future.

We almost died in the labour room. Unfortunately, both of us made it at the end. She took me in her arms for the first time and felt her resolve solidify. Despite everything that lied in front of her, she found a strength she never knew she possessed. From that day, she started fighting to live a normal life, for the three of us— my brother, herself and me.

She succeeded, more or less. My childhood was about studying, playing with my elder brother and being a chatty kid. Money was scarce, but my mother made all the happiness possible for us. "It's time for bed, who wants to listen to prince's stories?" my mother would call us softly, her voice like a sweet lullaby, soothing us to sleep. "Get up, you'll be late to school," she'd wake us up, caressing our faces. We'd wake up to the smell of her delicious breakfast.

My father was different in the mornings. Some days he would adore us. "Let's sing a song," he'd say, grinning, as we made up silly parodies and danced around. But some days, his mood would sour. "You ungrateful bastards! Sit down and be quiet," he'd bark suddenly, and we would freeze in our tracks, lowering our heads and obeying without a word till we disappeared in the background. One day, my father yelled at me for not filling a glass of water to his liking. "Why can't you do anything right? You swine!" he thundered. I stood there, tears streaming down my face, wondering what my mistake was. I think it was this unpredictable nature of my father that messed me up the most. If he was purely evil, I would still have accepted it. But he was neither here nor there.

"Hmmm… you've stood first in class again," my father said, a hint of rare pride in his voice. "This is what kids who are raised well do." I stood there, clutching the thin sheet of paper that dictated my worth. Warmth of his approval tinged my body knowing that this is a fleeting, momentary respite in a long, dry season. "People should know how well I have raised you." I nodded, forcing a smile, gathering courage to ask him, "Dad," I spoke in a whisper, afraid, "do you think I could try poetry…"

"No time for distractions. Concentrate on your medical entrance exams. I am not going to spend lakhs on your education. You will study further only if you get a scholarship or I will give away your worthless hands to the first person I see and send you off." He dismissed me with a wave to cut off any further thought. And just like that my love for those things labelled by him as trivial: poetry, art, music, dance— became a ghost of another life.

My brother took the first chance to escape this life. He was doing his Masters from another city and planned to get a job as far away from home as possible. But what about us? Were we destined to suffer at the hands of my father? Over time, I learned to keep a smiling face, despite my feelings. "How was your day?" my brother would ask when he called occasionally. "It was fine." I'd reply, no matter how the day was. But inside, I knew the truth. Everything wasn't fine. Nothing was fine. We were just playing a part in a facade of a perfect, happy family. I learnt to play along. But in the process of constantly playing this dual role, I don't remember when exactly I changed.

All these years, I also saw the woman who gave up her life for us. Her strength weakened a little after my brother left. The shade of exhaustion, helplessness below her eyes and frown between her brows grew from being a guest in her moments of despair to a permanent resident now. Drop by drop, her youth, her dreams, her happiness flowed from her eyes. But she continued her fight with her destiny, so my brother and I would not lose.

The most annoying part was that no one else saw him the way I did. He perfected his role of being an ideal and intellectual man. I pitied this tall, lanky guy, Alex, the most. He looked at my father with absolute adoration and took whatever bullshit he spewed. *How ironic,* I thought. It was as if nature was playing its little game again, *its game of balance.* We were opposites, I saw the reality, he believed the facade to be reality, both with utter dedication.

Alex was a college student when I first met him. He used to teach me and my brother to be able to afford his college fees. And now, he is all grown up, a practising lawyer with a wife and daughter. He is a good man, like the men of some *television drama*, he loved both of them dearly. He often paid a visit, sometimes even asked me about my transition from a chatty little girl to a secluded adult. I responded with nothing but a smile. I was a surgeon in the only hospital my city had now. I saw a lot of blood, bodies and broken bones daily. But the thing that disgusted me the most was the mere thought of someone that good, worshipping my trashy father.

One day, as I was reading Gorky's *Mother*, I heard a glass shatter. Dad had knocked a painting down. My heart leaped into my throat as I heard my father's angry cusses reverberating through the house followed by my mom's soft, pleading voice, trying to soothe him but it only fuelled his wild rage. I felt the familiar surge of fear, the instinct to flee and hide. The urge to make myself small and as invisible as possible. But something snapped inside me. I put the novel down and picked up the taser I had gotten in the self-defence kit. I trembled, stepping down the staircase, but I continued. My heart hammered in my chest. The sight that greeted me in the living room was the one I had seen too many times before: my mother, crying, crumpled on the floor, my father standing over her, his face twisted with anger. This time, I couldn't be a mere bystander.

"Stop!" my voice came out stronger than I thought, breaking the murky silence like a clap of thunder.

My father turned towards me, his eyes wild and unfocused with all the fury.

"You are not going to hurt her anymore," I said.

He laughed, in a cruel mocking way, "And? What are you going to do about it?"

I took a step forward, putting myself between him and my mom. She put a hand on my feet, pleading to run, save myself. I didn't want to. I saved myself enough. "Leave us alone," I said, my voice firm. He lifted his hand to slap me and right in that moment, I took out the taser and put it on his neck. I didn't stop till he was on the floor in front of me, unconscious. It was my time to laugh. I must admit it was an unsettling one, a little similar to my father's.

"What did you do?" my mother cried, "He'll kill us!"

"Go to your brother's place for a while mom. Trust me with this... just this once," I said, as our eyes glistened. I don't know why she believed me, but she did. She looked at dad one last time and then went inside her room to pack.

I looked at my dad and, for the first time in my life, I felt a certain calmness... and now that I had finally tasted it, I craved more of it. I tied him up and dropped him over the basement stairs. He was still unconscious just as I needed him to be.

Then it hit me, what if people start looking for him? That would soon lead them here. So, I went to his office the next day to ask around if anyone saw my father. Some Days later, I heard a knock on the door. It was Alex. He was not part of the original plan, but there he was, how could I leave him out.

"Hi. I hope you don't mind me dropping by like this," Alex said. "I've been trying to get in touch with your father, but I heard he is missing. Did you get any information?"

"No. He has not come home since Thursday. I asked around in his office. No one seems to know anything."

Alex sighed and ran a hand through his hair. "This is so unlike him. Anyways, how are you and aunty doing? Do you need anything?"

"No, we are good. Thank you for asking. He's always spoken highly of you. Maybe he's just taking a break. He has been under a lot of stress lately. I'll let you know as soon as he's back."

"Yes, I would like that. I have always admired him." He took a pause as if in trance. He continued after sometime, "Even I will try asking around. It's just...something doesn't feel right."

"Hmm. I just hope he'll be back soon."

"I hope so too." He nodded empathetically and left.

I closed the door behind me with a smirk and walked to the basement where my father was tied and gagged. I looked at him with a mix of contempt and determination.

"Alex is worried about you. I told him you'll be back soon."

He struggled against the restraints.

"Not now. First you need to see what you have created. You need to see the results of the damage you have done. Now, that will take some time won't it, father? Just relax." I left him that day, suffering in anticipation of what may happen next.

I woke him up by throwing ice water on his face. Sleep was a luxury I didn't want him to have. He jostled awake and looked at me, trying to look for a daughter who wasn't there.

I fetched the small blade from my pocket after tightly securing the gag in his mouth. As much as I wanted to hear him scream, I did not want him to have the freedom to scream. My mother did not have the freedom to express when she was hurting. Why should he?

At first, I just played around with the blade, I relished the pleasing sight of his eyes going wide with fear and hope dying a very satisfying death. I took his hand and made a small cut, nothing too deep, just enough to draw some blood. And then another, and another and another while listening to the calming melody of his choked screams. I saw the veins, delicate blue-green threads pulsing beneath the skin, with one swift cut, there was a satisfactory rivulet of crimson peeking out. He twitched with each new gash, trying to wiggle out of his tightly bound limbs. His screams shifted from cries to desperate ragged gasps barely audible over the sound of my blade gliding across his skin. His skin slowly became a tapestry of deep and shallow jagged lines, each one oozing with life, his sins painted across every inch. After one point, the sounds he made faded into the background. All I could see were the beautiful red beads forming and freezing on his skin. It was beautiful. Like poetry crafted on a body.

Alex dropped by again. He was still looking for my dad, and wanted to know if I heard anything. We had an interesting conversation after that. There came a point where I said, "You know Alex, it's fascinating how some people can weave such an intricate web of lies. Like the lead in the movie *Focus*. He is a con artist who teaches the girl that the trick is in distracting people and making them focus on one point, so you can steal something from elsewhere. So much has been stolen because the focus was diverted to the wrong place.

"That's an interesting observation, I haven't watched the movie. But I don't understand the context."

Why are people so dumb. "Nothing, just random thoughts. Oh, I almost forgot. I have something to give you." I got up to get his camera from the other room. "Here, I found it while cleaning today. I am sorry, we should have returned it long back."

He smiled, "It's alright, it's not that I use it that regularly either. Seems like the battery is dead. Did I give you the charger?"

"Nope, just the camera."

"Oh okay, then I will ask my wife. She is particular about keeping things in order, she must know."

"How is she by the way? Mom used to love her visits. But then she just stopped coming one day."

"Yeah. She is just busy with the kid I guess. She doesn't really have time for anything else."

"Understandable. Anyways, give her my regards. I will let you know if I get to know something about dad."

Things were falling into place better than I imagined. All I had to do was wait.

Dad was doing great. I got a supply of his favourite brand and gave him just enough and teased him with the rest. Alcohol eases pain, and now that would just be counterproductive now, won't it?

I was visiting him after two days and the stench was overpowering— A rotten mix of sweat, dried blood, and my father's shitty persona. No matter how he came home, he made sure to clean up in the mornings to make a good impression. One day he was angry at mom for not being able to remove stains from his white shirt properly. He first beat her up till she bled into her clothes and made her wash them with hot salt water. His screams now bring back the memory of my mother's dread. I wonder if sitting in boiling salt water would do the same trick on his blooded clothes. We will find out.

I held a metal pot of boiling salt water above him, watching his dazed eyes trying to focus on the fumes. Fear finally sat in and I saw my father wetting his pants.

"Wh…Why are you doing this to me?" he groaned.

"You still don't know? And I always assumed you were intelligent." I moved closer to him. "I learnt all this from you, father. I am just doing everything you did to mom and me. Don't you remember?" I whispered, pouring a slow trickle onto his shirt. The scalding water hissed against his skin and he howled— a high-pitched sound that caressed my heart. He fainted. *Now that's rude.* I forced him awake. "Talk to me, you can't avoid this conversation by fainting?

He could not even hold his head up for long. "Look at me. Marvel at what you have created." He did not. He could not. I slapped him, hard, feeling the wet slap of blood on my hand, leaving a smear that felt almost satisfying. "You owe me this!" I pulled his collar and shook him awake. He kept quiet for the first time.

I sat in silence in the empty house, reminiscing how this womanizing bastard shattered everything of what we could have been. I felt a sudden urge for another visit. Still had a little bit of settlement of pain. After all, I didn't know how long it would take for Alex to figure out how this trash screwed his trust. *Till then, the prey was mine.*

"Hi dad! How are you doing?" I asked, ripping the tape off his mouth.

"Bitch."

"Good to see you too. Looks like you've been enjoying my arrangements for your accommodation."

"Alex wants to see you badly. What do you think he will do when he finds out how you betrayed his trust?" His eyes widened with terror and his abuses quieted into silence.

I slowly walked around him, savouring every moment. The basement, dimly lit, added to the feeling of darkness in me. The only source of light was a flickering bulb hanging from the ceiling, casting long shadows on his face, highlighting the sweat and dried blood that mixed into a beautiful canvas of suffering.

"Do you remember making her cry? Making her shed blood tears? Snatching everything away from her and treating her like dirt?" I spat out.

"I am sorry, I didn't..."

"Sorry?" I laughed, "You crushed her whole life under your toe... you ruined us all... Did you ever bother thinking about what we went through? I know, you didn't. But now you will."

I took out a small vial and syringe. "This won't kill you. It'll just paralyse you. You will feel every pain I will inflict; you just won't be able to do anything about it."

His eyes widened in panic, "No, You can't do that!!"

He clearly didn't know me well enough to say that.

"Try me" I said joyfully as I injected the neurotoxin. His eyes filled with tears and his breath quickened, but gradually he grew stiff and lost control of his body except for his eyeballs which danced around, struggling to focus on me, till they shut.

Over the next few weeks, I fed him and allowed all the wounds to heal. Just enough for him to be able to walk and look like himself again. His mind, however, was going to take a lot more time. But he did not have that kind of time, I saw to that.

One day, I called Alex, "Hey, I just wanted to let you know that dad came back. He does not seem like himself. But at least he is home."

And as I anticipated, Alex came. His eyes were red with anger. One look at him, and I understood he saw what was on that camera. He sat in front of my father, trying to search for his mentor, but all he saw was the man who betrayed his trust. He stood up to leave.

What? He won't do anything? What's wrong with him?

He stopped, looked at me, looked at my dad then it happened way too fast. His fist, my dad's jaw, then dad was on the floor.

Now that's what I'm talking about. You did not disappoint.

Alex stormed out. I called the police. I got what I needed.

I told the police about what happened. "Sir, Alex has been a family friend for years. He was my teacher. When my dad went missing, he asked me to let him know about his return. If I knew he would kill my father, I would never..." And that was the cue for the waterworks.

It was a straightforward case of assault and murder. The police her have always been too lazy to dig deep. They found a body of an old man on the floor. I was the eye witness, who told them about who did it. They believed. Alex could not deny what he did. He did hit the man. He had the motive and the occasion. Cased solved. Case closed.

My brother and mother were called home for his funeral. They were told what happened, they did not want to know more either. They were just relieved that they were free from the monster. We cremated him, nothing remained now— no body, no autopsy, no case.

Things have been different at home since. A few moons ago my brother returned to his world, we did not mind. I liked it this way, just mom and me. Today was a cozy day. It was raining outside. I made tea, and we sat at the window just being present in the moment. It was good to see her carefree. A sense of satisfaction coursed through me. All my life, I had dreamt of experiencing such calmness. This was different from what I felt hurting my father. This feeling was something different, and it came only when my mother's smile returned to its full, radiant glory. She was finally free. Free from the shadows of fear and pain. She whispered a small "thank you" and we hugged to our heart's content. That moment, that feeling, that was the greatest joy for me.

Call for Submissions

Theme: Friendship

Friends are the family we choose for ourselves. Some friends are limited to certain aspects of our lives, some are college friends, some are travelling friends, some become friends in the most random fashion, but all of them hold a special place.

We invite you to submit your stories and tell us about any special encounter with your friend. It could be the moment you decided to be friends, or a moment you could not have survived without that friend, or moments you would probably not have if not for that friend.

Submission Guidelines:

Please submit your stories as an editable Word document.

There is no age limit to be an author.

Language: English

Word Limit: 2000- 5000 words

Font: Times New Roman, 12

Spacing: 1.5

Deadline: 31st July 2025

Manuscripts will be reviewed within a month from the deadline of submission (by August 31st)

Authors can expect to hear from us with one of the following

responses: Accepted, Revision Required, Submission Declined.

There is **no submission or publication charges.**

We currently cannot offer payments for the stories published. However, along with the recognition as a published author; as our generous thanks to the authors of the selected stories, we would be offering a small reward in the form of a gift.

Looking forward to hearing from you!

For submissions or any queries regarding submissions, feel free to send us an email: sv.shortfiction@gmail.com

www.ingramcontent.com/pod-product-compliance
Lightning Source LLC
Chambersburg PA
CBHW031311130726
47988CB00007B/2802